# What's happening to me?

Susan Meredith

Designed & illustrated by Nancy Leschnikoff

Edited by Jane Chisholm

Consultants: Dr. Jeremy Kirk, Revd Professor Michael J. Reiss & Katie Kirk, RSCN, RHV

# Contents

# Growing up

You've been growing up little by little ever since you were born, but there's a time when you'll start to alter a lot. That's when you begin to change from a child into an adult, and it's what this book is all about.

You might have noticed some changes happening to you already, or maybe there haven't been any yet. They don't happen to everyone at the same age and you can't tell in advance when they'll happen to you. But read the next few pages and you'll get some idea of what to expect, and when.

Perhaps you're looking forward to growing up, or maybe you have doubts. Don't worry – the changes take place gradually, so you'll have plenty of time to get used to them.

This new phase in your life is called puberty, and it's nature's way of getting you ready to have babies when you're older. You can read all about that in this book too.

Growing up is easier if you take good care of yourself. Towards the end of the book, you'll find tips for doing just that, including eating well, getting exercise and coping with other people.

# When will it happen?

People usually say you start changing when you're about 10, but it happens to some girls earlier than this and to others quite a bit later. The most usual age for the first changes is between 8 and 13. The fact is, when your body is ready, you'll start growing up.

## Your weight

First of all, you have to build up some fat. Your body needs this as an energy store before it can cope with all the changes. So don't worry if you put on a bit of weight. It's not bad for you.

## Same age, different stage

You might be the same age as your friend, but that doesn't mean you'll be growing up at exactly the same time. You may have finished growing and developing before she's even started, or the other way round. This can be embarrassing for both of you. If you start changing young, you may feel proud of your new body, but you might also feel self-conscious about being ahead of everyone else. If you don't start changing until later, you can feel left out, and as though everyone still treats you like a child when you don't want to be one.

You can't make yourself grow up faster, or more slowly. But one thing's for sure – everyone gets to the same stage in the end. No matter how old you are when you start puberty, you'll go on changing until you're fully grown up.

4

# What next?

Just so you know what to expect, here's a list of growing-up changes in the order they usually happen. But it doesn't matter if the order is different for you. Many will overlap anyway.

You get taller, broader and heavier.

Your breasts start to develop.

Your face gets longer.

Your pubic hair starts to grow.

Hair grows under your arms.

You start to sweat more.

Your skin and hair may get greasier.

Your sex organs develop.

Your periods start.

## A new you

It can take up to 3½ years from the very first changes of puberty to starting your periods. And it will be several more years after that before you finish growing up. All along, you'll start to feel a bit different in yourself. You're changing mentally as well as physically, and this can be stressful sometimes. Don't worry though; you'll still be you at the end of it all – just a more grown-up version of yourself.

Me, age 5

# Taller and wider

When everyone starts telling you how much you've grown, the chances are that other changes are on the way too. Getting taller quickly is one of the very earliest signs of puberty. Soon after you start growing upwards, you'll start broadening out as well.

Not all girls have a really obvious growth spurt. Some seem to grow more gradually over several years.

## A growth spurt

Girls usually grow fastest around the time they're 11½, but you may grow tall when you're quite a bit younger or older than this. Most girls have almost finished growing by the time they're 15.

If you go through a growth spurt early, it's likely that you'll stop growing early too. And if you start your growth spurt later, you may well catch up the early growers and even overtake them.

# The broad bits

Your hips will be the part of you to broaden out the most. The bones of your pelvis widen to make more room for babies to grow inside you and be born.

## Muscle power

Adults have twice as much muscle as babies, and you build up most of the extra during puberty. That's one good reason to eat well and do some exercise now.

Girls tend to have less strength than boys, but not only because they're naturally less muscley. Boys are usually bigger, with broader shoulders and bigger hearts and lungs.

## The weight question

You'll get a lot heavier, maybe doubling your weight between the ages of 9 and 18. It isn't only fat and muscles that cause this; your bigger bones also weigh more and so do internal organs such as your heart and liver.

Girls put on more fat than boys, but for a reason. The extra can be used for energy when a woman is pregnant and breast-feeding her babies.

# Getting hairy

One of the first changes you'll notice is that you start getting hair in places you didn't have it before. Some people don't like this very much, but at least no one else needs to see it.

## Pubic hair

The first hair to sprout is your pubic hair. This gets more curly as it grows, and it may be a different colour from the hair on your head. If the hair gets so bushy that it sticks out from your swimsuit, you can always trim it; but, to save your skin, use round-ended baby scissors, not sharp ones.

Pubic hair grows in a triangle shape here.

## What's the hair for?

No one really knows why people get pubic and armpit hair. Weirdly, it may be to give sweat something to cling to. Many animals use their sweaty smell to attract a mate, but this doesn't seem to work in humans.

# Under your arms

About a year after you get pubic hair, you'll notice hair starts growing in your armpits too. If you want to shave this hair (you don't have to), you'll need a razor and some shaving foam or gel from a chemist's or supermarket.

 1. First, splash some warm water on your armpits, then squeeze on a little bit of foam and spread it over the hair with your finger. Make sure the razor blade is securely in place.

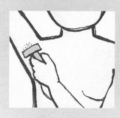 2. Carefully shave the hair off. Go downwards first, rinse your blade in water, then shave upwards to finish off. Rinse your armpits with cold water and dry them. Wait a few minutes before you put deodorant on, or it will sting.

If your skin feels sore after shaving, it may be that your blade is blunt or that you're sensitive to the foam you're using.

# On your legs

You might see more hair on your legs, but that's normal too. Humans are related to apes and the first people who ever lived were probably very hairy indeed. It's easy to cut yourself shaving your legs. If you do shave, go slowly and carefully in an upwards direction, and don't go higher than you need.

# Getting breasts

Why do you get breasts anyway? Well, they're mainly for feeding any babies you might have, as breast milk is a baby's healthiest first food. Most people think they look attractive too and they're sensitive to being touched.

## Sooner or later

If you start getting breasts young, it doesn't mean they'll end up being big. They'll probably stop growing early too. And if you're a late developer, you won't necessarily have small breasts. They may carry on growing until you're about 17.

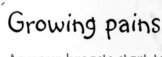

Ow!

## Growing pains

As your breasts start to grow, they might feel a bit tender, tingly or itchy, but this will soon wear off. One breast may grow faster than the other, but don't worry about ending up lopsided. They will even out, although no one has exactly symmetrical breasts.

## How breasts work

Breasts are made mostly of fat, which cushions and protects the milk-making areas deep inside. Milk isn't made until a woman has had a baby. It comes out of the nipples through tiny holes that are too small to see.

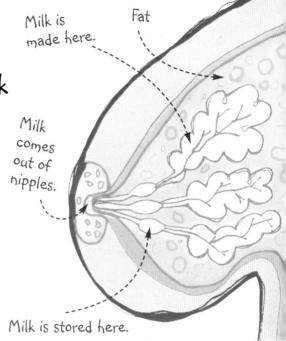

Milk is made here.

Fat

Milk comes out of nipples.

Milk is stored here.

## All shapes and sizes

A lot of girls, and women too, feel self-conscious about their breasts. They come in such different sizes, it's easy to worry that you should be bigger or smaller than you are. But small, medium-sized and big breasts are all quite normal. And the good thing is, different people find different sizes attractive.

# The bra business

It's really up to you when you start wearing a bra. Bras are made even for people with the tiniest breasts. On the other hand, if you don't like the idea, you don't have to wear a bra at all, although most women find it more comfortable when they're doing exercise.

## Measuring up

It's a help to have a rough idea of your size before you go to buy a bra. Here's how to measure yourself.

1. Measure round your ribcage, just below your breasts. Pull the tape measure tight to do this. Then add on 12cm (5in). This gives you your chest size: e.g.

   68cm (27in) + 12cm (5in) = 80cm (32in).

2. Now measure around the fullest part of your breasts, across the nipples. Don't flatten them with the tape measure.

   ✳ If this measurement is the same as your chest size, you are an AA cup.

   ✳ If there is a 10-15mm (½in) difference, you are an A cup.

   ✳ A 2.5cm (1in) difference means you are a B cup.

   ✳ A 5cm (2in) difference makes you a C cup.

   ✳ A 7.5cm (3in) difference and you are a D cup.

# The right fit

The only way to find a bra that really fits is to try on lots of different styles and even makes. The bra should fit tightly round your ribs so it can't ride up. And the cups shouldn't be so big that they wrinkle, or so tight that you bulge out. Put your top on to check the bra gives you a good shape under your clothes.

# Types of bra

"First" or "teen" bras are made to be soft and comfortable. They usually cover your breasts completely, aren't too transparent and give you a natural shape.

A sports bra should hold your breasts in position and keep you cool while you exercise.

Under T-shirts, smooth bras, without lots of seams and decoration, look best.

With a multiway bra, you can alter the straps so they don't show when you're wearing a halterneck or other style top.

Underwired bras give more support and shape to larger breasts but aren't recommended for under-16-year-olds. They may be bad for breasts that are still developing.

My first bra!

# How does it start?

So how do all these changes come about? Something has to trigger them off, then keep them going. It's all to do with chemical messengers called hormones. You have many different hormones in your body. But at puberty you get a lot more of some of them, especially the ones called sex hormones.

## All in the head

You can't make sex hormones until your brain gives the right signal to your body. One night, while you're asleep, a grape-sized part of your brain, called your hypothalamus, starts to make a hormone known as GnRH. Once there is enough GnRH, another part of your brain, called the pituitary, knows it's time to make two other new hormones: FSH and LH.

Although there's all this activity in your brain, you won't notice anything. The real action begins once FSH and LH send their signal to another part of your body entirely – your ovaries, which are in your tummy. These will start making lots of sex hormones and that's when you'll notice big changes.

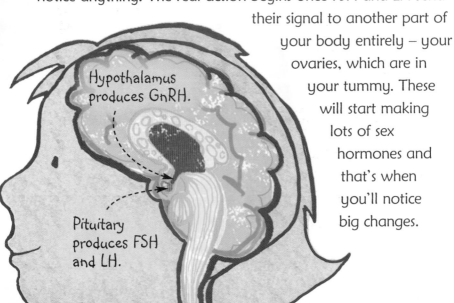

Hypothalamus produces GnRH.

Pituitary produces FSH and LH.

# Sex hormones

There are two main sex hormones for girls: oestrogen and progesterone. Oestrogen brings about some changes, like getting breasts, for example. Progesterone has a lot to do with periods (see pages 22-29).

# How hormones work

Hormones travel in your blood to the places they need to reach. They are made in endocrine glands in your body. Your hypothalamus and pituitary are both examples of endocrine glands. So are your ovaries, where the sex hormones, oestrogen and progesterone, are made. You can find out more about your ovaries on pages 18-19.

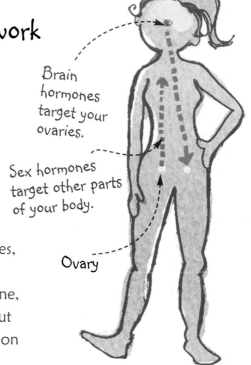

Brain hormones target your ovaries.

Sex hormones target other parts of your body.

Ovary

# Male or female?

Female sex hormones aren't exclusive to girls – boys have some too. And girls have some male sex hormones, including the main one, which is called testosterone. Maybe girls and boys aren't so very different after all.

# What's it all about?

Why do you have to change at all? Basically, it's so you can have babies when you're older. But your body can produce babies long before you could enjoy having one or could look after one properly.

## How does sex work?

For a baby to start, a sperm from a man's body has to meet and join together with an ovum (egg) in a woman's body. For this to happen, a woman and a man have sex. First, they usually cuddle each other very close.

Sperm

The man's penis (his willy) gets stiffer and the woman's vagina releases a bit of slippery fluid. Her vagina is a tube with the opening between her legs. The man's penis fits inside it. A small amount of fluid called semen comes out of the man's penis. It contains millions of sperm, which swim up into the woman's body. If they meet an egg, one of them may join with it and a baby may start growing.

Only one sperm can join with an egg.

## Lots of eggs

You have all the eggs you will ever need right from birth. At puberty, they start maturing enough to develop into babies.

An egg is really the size of a tiny dot. Sperm are even smaller.

# Pregnancy myths

You might hear about babies
being brought by storks or found under gooseberry
bushes. But there's only one way for a baby to start –
that's when sperm from a man's penis come into contact
with a woman's vagina. And, by the way, you can't get
pregnant on your own, or from kissing or holding hands.

# Sex and feelings

Couples don't have sex only to make babies. It can be a
way of showing deep affection for each other, which is
why it's also called "making love". Sex can make people
feel very good, but it can also make them feel very bad
if they do it with someone they don't especially like, or
when they don't really want to.

# Sex without babies

If a couple don't want to have a baby, they can take
precautions to stop the woman becoming pregnant
when they have sex. The precautions are known as
contraception. One method is for the couple to use a
condom. This is a thin cover which they put onto the
man's penis before it goes into the woman's vagina.
The semen gets caught in the end of the condom
so the sperm don't reach an egg.

A condom ------→

# The changes inside you ...

For your body to get ready for having babies, big changes need to happen in what are called your sex organs. You won't really notice the changes as most of your sex organs are tucked away inside your body.

Your sex organs are low down in your tummy.

## What everything is for

You have two ovaries, two fallopian tubes, a womb (sometimes called a uterus), a cervix and a vagina. These will all get bigger, just like the rest of you.

Your ovaries are where your eggs are stored. When your ovaries are full-grown, they are about the size and shape of walnuts.

The hollow part of your fallopian tubes is only about as wide as the lead in a pencil. This is where a sperm may meet and join with an egg if a couple have sex.

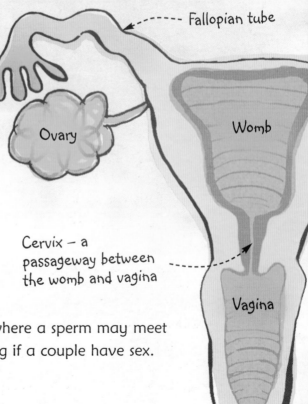

Fallopian tube

Ovary

Womb

Cervix – a passageway between the womb and vagina

Vagina

## Where everything is

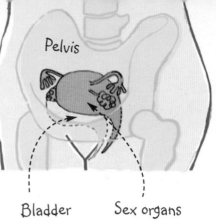

Pelvis

Your sex organs (shown on the right in red) are behind and just above your bladder, where urine (wee) is stored. They are protected by the bones of your pelvis.

Bladder        Sex organs

Fallopian tube

Ovary

If a woman becomes pregnant, the baby grows inside her womb. A womb is normally about the size and shape of an upside-down, hollowed-out pear. It stretches hugely as a baby gets bigger.

Your vagina is a tube which leads to the outside of your body. It is about 10cm (4in) long and its walls are very stretchy. A man's penis fits inside a woman's vagina during sex and babies travel down it to leave their mother's body and be born.

This diagram shows the route sperm take to the fallopian tubes, where they might meet an egg from an ovary.

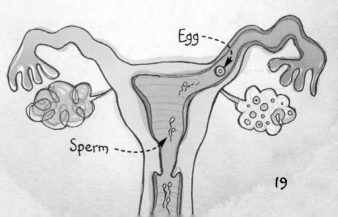

Egg

Sperm

19

# ... and on the outside

Sex organs that are on the outside of your body are called genitals. Girls' genitals aren't very obvious. In fact, you can't really see them unless you use a mirror.

## The vulva

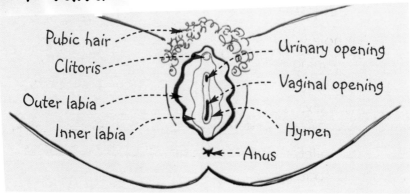

The proper word for girls' genitals is vulva.

Your vulva is cushioned by two thick folds of skin called the outer labia (lips). Don't worry if yours aren't symmetrical.

Inside the outer labia you have two smaller lips called the inner labia. These are sensitive to touch.

At the front, where your inner labia meet, is a small pea-shaped bump called the clitoris. This is very sensitive to touch.

The vaginal opening stretches easily, like the vagina itself.

Your vaginal opening may be covered by a thin layer of skin called the hymen. Often this wears away while you're a child, especially if you do a lot of sport. It will wear away completely as you grow.

Have a look in a mirror if you want to. `-----→`

# Nearby parts

The tiny hole where your urine comes out, called the urinary opening, is a bit further back than your clitoris. It isn't really part of your genitals because it has nothing to do with sex.

Your anus (where the solid waste comes out when you go to the toilet) isn't part of your vulva either, but it's very close to it.

# Bodily fluids

As you grow up, fluid starts leaking out of your vaginal opening sometimes. This might sound off-putting but it's actually healthy, as the fluid keeps your vagina clean and moisturized. There won't be so much of it that it soaks through your knickers.

# Same but different

When they're in their mother's womb, girl and boy babies look the same at first. It's only after about 12 weeks that their genitals start to develop differently. The pea-shaped part that becomes a clitoris in girls goes on to grow into a penis in boys.

# Why periods happen

The biggest growing-up change of all is that you start having periods – a few days of slight bleeding each month from your vagina. This might sound scary, but periods show that your body is working properly. If you know what to expect, they're nothing to worry about.

## Periods and babies

Periods are all to do with babies. Every month, a woman's womb builds up a thick, soft lining of blood vessels, so that a baby could nestle there and grow. When the woman doesn't become pregnant, the womb lining breaks down and comes out of her vagina as a period.

People usually notice a period has started when they go to the toilet.

Guess what? I've started!

## When periods start

There are a couple of clues to when your periods might start. It will probably be about 2½ years after your breasts begin to grow. And for a few months before your first period, you might get more fluid than usual leaking out of your vagina. Periods usually start sometime between the ages of 10 and 15 – but not always.

# How often, how long?

The time between the start of one period and the start of the next is often about 28 days (4 weeks or about a month). But this can vary, from 20 to 35 days or even longer, especially when your periods first begin. And each period can last as little as 2 days or as long as 8.

# All caused by hormones

It's your sex hormones that make your periods happen. In the first half of the month, oestrogen makes the lining of your womb thicken up. Then, a ripe egg bursts out of one of your ovaries and travels down a fallopian tube.

Womb lining starts getting thicker.

Egg is sucked into fallopian tube.

Progesterone now thickens the womb lining even more. But when the egg doesn't meet a sperm and start growing into a baby, the egg breaks down, and the levels of oestrogen and progesterone fall. This makes the lining break down, and your period starts.

Lining about 5mm thick

Egg has died away and period has started.

# Using towels

Most girls feel happier using sanitary towels (pads) instead of tampons when they first start their periods. Sanitary towels fit in your knickers and soak up the blood as it leaves your body.

## Types of towels

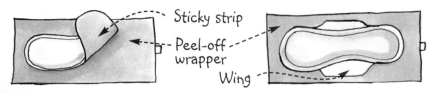

Sticky strip
Peel-off wrapper
Wing

Most towels have a sticky strip on the back and you press them onto your knickers to hold them in place. It might take a bit of practice to get them in exactly the right position each time.

Some towels have side flaps too, known as wings. These fold over and stick to the underneath of your knickers, so the towel is held in place extra securely and is a bit more absorbent too.

## Size and thickness

Towels come in different sizes, so you can choose one to fit the shape of your body. They come in different thicknesses too. The blood usually flows more heavily near the start of your period, so you might need a thicker towel then, and at bedtime, when you won't be changing it until the morning.

# Changing towels

You'll soon get used to feeling when your towel needs changing. In the day, you should change towels every few hours anyway – not just in case they leak, but also to stop bacteria building up on them. Period blood is completely clean, but once it's outside your body it meets bacteria in the air and this can cause a smell or even infections.

# Getting rid of towels

You can't flush towels down the toilet, as they block the pipes, or sometimes end up polluting beaches or rivers. Instead, you need to wrap them up and put them in a bin. If your towels are individually wrapped, you can put them back in their wrapper to throw away; otherwise, use an old plastic bag. It's a good idea to take a bag with you when you go out, although special bins are often provided in public toilets and you may not need bags to use those.

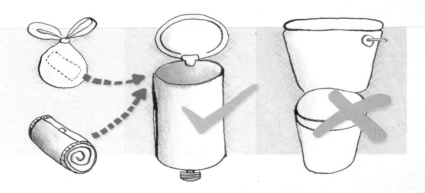

# Using tampons

Many women prefer tampons to sanitary towels because they soak up period blood right inside your vagina and you can't feel a tampon once it's in place. There's no risk at all of tampons being seen through your clothes and you can even go swimming with one in.

## Types of tampons

Some tampons come with an applicator designed to help you get the tampon into your vagina.

Some people find it easier to use the non-applicator type of tampon which you just push in with your finger.

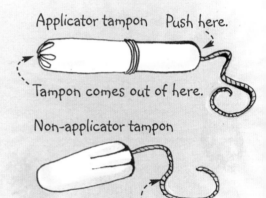

Applicator tampon    Push here.

Tampon comes out of here.

Non-applicator tampon

String for pulling tampon out. You leave it outside your body.

## Size

Tampons come in different sizes. The size you use depends on how heavy your period is, not on the size of your body. Some packs have a few tampons of different sizes in them, for different days of your period.

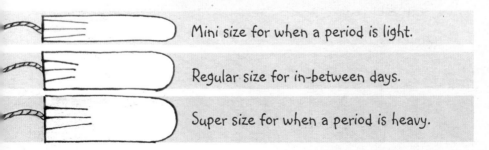

Mini size for when a period is light.

Regular size for in-between days.

Super size for when a period is heavy.

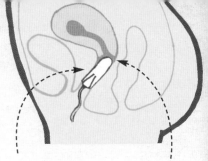

# Putting a tampon in

It's best to try a tampon for the first time when your period is heavy, as it will go in more easily. Use a small size, and follow the instructions carefully. If you can't get it in, it's probably just that you're tense. Leave it for now and try another time.

The tampon should slope backwards.

It needs to be high in your vagina so you don't feel it. Your cervix stops it going too far up.

# Changing tampons

Just as a tampon starts to leak, you might feel a bubbling sensation and the string will get bloodstained. Even if your period is light, you need to change tampons every four hours or sooner. If you don't, vaginal bacteria can cause infection. For this reason, it can be a good idea to use a towel at night.

Tampons will flush away, but it's better for the environment if you get rid of them in the same way as towels.

# To use or not to use?

You can try tampons even if you've only just started your periods, so long as you feel comfortable about it. But read the instructions carefully, especially the part about toxic shock syndrome. This is a rare but serious illness. To reduce your risk, use the smallest tampons you can, change them often, and use towels at night or when your period is very light.

# Coping with periods

Having periods is a normal, healthy part of growing up, and many people have no problems with them at all. On the other hand, your hormone levels are going up and down throughout the month and this can make you feel better at some times than others.

## Period pain

Some women get an ache low down in their tummy at the start of a period. This happens when hormones affect muscles in the womb.

Doing some exercise often helps a lot, but if the pain is too bad for that, you can try resting for a while with a hot-water bottle on your tummy. If that doesn't work either, you may be able to take a painkiller.

## PMS

Some people feel bloated, headachey, tired and low for a few days before their period. This is known as PMS (premenstrual syndrome) and is probably caused by changing hormone levels. There's no foolproof remedy, but it's worth trying to eat healthy food little and often throughout the day, as well as taking exercise and getting extra sleep.

# Top tips

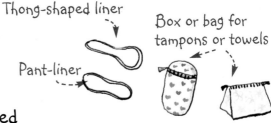

Thong-shaped liner

Pant-liner

Box or bag for tampons or towels

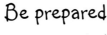

### Be prepared

As your periods may not be regular at first, carry a towel or tampon with you, just in case. You can also wear a pant-liner when you're expecting a period. These are like very small, thin pads. In an emergency, use tissues, paper towels, toilet paper or even a sock.

### Be confident

You may feel that everyone can tell you're having a period just by looking at you. They really can't. And most towels are so slim they would never be seen unless your clothes were really skintight.

### Change towels and tampons often

Some people wear dark-coloured clothes during their period just in case of a leak. If the worst happens, try tying your jumper round your waist to hide the mark, or turn your skirt round so people will think you've spilled something down your front.

### Relax in a bath

Blood flows more slowly in water, so it's fine to have a bath. Just have lots of toilet paper ready afterwards, so you don't get blood on your bath towel.

# Your feelings

It's not surprising if you sometimes get moody – you're changing so fast, emotionally as well as physically. Don't despair. Your hormones still have to find their level, but they'll settle down eventually and, then, so will you.

## Friends

You might find that some of your childhood friendships shift around a bit, as you all grow up at different rates and perhaps develop new interests. It's usual to want to belong to a group of friends, but don't feel you always have to follow the group. True friends will respect you for being an individual too.

If you often feel shy and awkward, it may help to know that lots of other people do too. Even the loudest types can be covering up a lack of confidence inside.

## Parents

It's normal to become less dependent on your parents. That's how you prepare to fend for yourself as an adult. But it often causes disagreements. Your parents will want to protect you from making bad decisions, because you haven't had much experience of life yet. Keep talking things over with them, and compromising – they probably only want you to be safe and happy. As they realize you're becoming more mature, the chances are they'll allow you more independence.

# Fancying people

As you get older, it's only natural to start feeling sexually attracted to other people. You might even fantasize about someone you fancy. But don't worry – that's a safe way of exploring your emotions. And touching your genitals because it feels good (called masturbation) is natural too. Masturbating might end in an orgasm (often called "coming") – this is a fluttery, shuddery feeling in your genitals that can make your whole body feel relaxed.

The age when people want to start dating varies, just like all the other changes of growing up. Don't feel pressured to go out with anyone until you're ready to, and don't date anyone unless they treat you with kindness and respect.

It isn't unusual to fancy someone the same sex as you when you're growing up. Usually, people go on to have stronger feelings for the opposite sex, but this doesn't always happen. And it's possible to fancy both boys and girls.

Women who date other women are known as lesbians. The word "gay" is more often used to describe men who date men, but can be used to describe lesbians too.

# Good food

Believe it or not, you really will deal with the ups and downs of puberty better if you're eating a good diet. You won't just feel healthier and more energetic, but your hair and skin will look healthier too.
And you'll be more likely to reach a good weight and stay at it.

## Food groups

You have to eat lots of different foods to get all the nutrients (goodness) you need. Dieticians divide food into five groups.

### 1. Bread, potatoes, rice, pasta and cereals
These are starchy carbohydrates and you should eat lots, for energy.

### 2. Fruit and vegetables (fresh, frozen or canned)
Eat at least five portions a day. These give you essential vitamins and minerals, as well as fibre, which helps protect you from diseases. (Potatoes aren't included in this group, but beans and lentils are.)

### 3. Meat, fish, eggs, nuts, beans, lentils
Eat moderate amounts of these foods. They provide protein, which helps you to grow.

### 4. Milk, cheese, yogurt
Eat moderate amounts. These foods contain calcium, which helps you to develop strong bones and teeth.

### 5. Foods containing fat and/or sugar
Don't eat too many of these. Examples of foods that are mostly fat and sugar include milk shakes, ice cream and biscuits.

# How much?

At puberty, you need as much food as an adult woman because you're growing so fast. Hunger is the best guide to how much to eat – eat when you're hungry, but don't keep eating once you're full. And don't worry about putting on a bit of weight. As you grow taller, you'll appear slimmer again.

This chart shows what proportion of your food should come from each group. You should eat most from groups 1 and 2 and least from group 5.

# More about eating

## Breakfast

Don't skip breakfast. Your body
uses energy even while you're
asleep and you need to replace it
in the morning. A healthy
breakfast stops you feeling weak
and sluggish, improves your
concentration and makes you
function better all round.

## Food and teeth

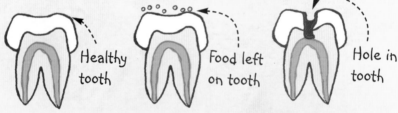

Healthy
tooth

Food left
on tooth

Hole in
tooth

You will have your adult teeth by the time you're about 13
and they have to last you for life. If food specks are left on
them, the teeth will eventually get holes in them.

You need to brush thoroughly twice a day, especially
before you go to bed. Brush up and down to dislodge food
from between the teeth, and learn how to floss. If you have
a brace, follow your orthodontist's
advice – sugary food and drink is
bad for all teeth but will rot teeth
with braces double-quick.

Angle your brush like this to
clean the backs of your teeth.

# Ready meals versus fresh

The food in most ready meals has been altered in some way in a factory. In this processing, nutrients may have been lost and substances such as artificial colourings and sweeteners may have been added. Some researchers think these can cause ill health, and dieticians generally recommend eating food which is as fresh and unprocessed as possible.

# Junk food

Junk food is food that has very little or no goodness in it. Usually it contains a lot of sugar, fat or salt, and is often fattening too. Examples of junk food are sugary drinks, sweets, lollies, bought biscuits and cakes, and salted snacks, including crisps. It's hard to avoid junk completely, but just try to have healthy snacks such as fruit whenever you can.

# Eating disorders

Eating disorders are serious illnesses triggered by emotional problems, not by food itself. Sufferers from anorexia don't eat enough, believing they are fat when they are not. Sufferers from bulimia binge eat, then make themselves vomit for fear of getting fat. Anyone who may be developing an eating disorder should tell an adult they trust straightaway – it's easier to recover if any medical treatment starts early.

# Keep moving

Exercise makes you feel more energetic, physically and mentally. It also helps you to sleep, reduces stress, makes you look good, and helps you stay at a healthy weight. It even has long-term benefits too, helping to prevent illnesses from heart disease to depression.

## Why now?

Your body's meant to be used so don't fall into the trap of giving up exercise at puberty. This is the very time you need it to build up muscles (including your heart) and strong bones. It's harder to do this when you're older. You might find it difficult to motivate yourself at first, but it will get easier once you notice how good you feel after exercising.

## How much?

To get fit and stay fit, you really need to exercise for at least half an hour a day (preferably an hour). This sounds a lot but it can include walking to school, as long as you walk fast. At least twice a week your exercise needs to be fairly strenuous – it should get your heart beating fast.

36

# What kind?

Stamina, suppleness and strength – these are the three Ss you need to develop for all-round fitness. (Stamina is the ability to keep doing something without getting tired.) Examples of sports that are good for all three Ss include energetic dancing, football, ice-skating, rollerblading, swimming and tennis. But any exercise is better than none and if there's a sport you want to try, go ahead and do it – you're more likely to stick at something you enjoy.

Cycling

Martial arts

Horse riding

Energetic dancing

Fast walking

Rollerblading

Gymnastics

Football

Swimming

Skateboarding

Tennis

Ice-skating

# Rest and sleep

Puberty is hard work for your body and your mind, so you need time to rest and recover. While you're asleep, your body repairs itself, and your dreams may help you to learn and make sense of things that have happened to you. Most 8-10-year-olds need about 10 hours sleep a night, and most 11-15-year-olds need about 9 hours.

# Keep clean

You'll need to wash a bit more now than you did when you were younger if you want to stay smelling sweet. This isn't because you get dirtier, but because you start to sweat more.

## Washing

You have sweat glands all over your skin but they're more concentrated in some areas – in your armpits and around your genitals. Even if you can't always have a shower, you need to wash those bits every day to stop smells developing. And you may need to change your clothes more often than you used to, at least your underwear and tops.

## Deodorants

Most "deodorants" have an antiperspirant in them too. Deodorants work by stopping smells developing on your sweat, while antiperspirants actually cut down on how much you sweat. A deodorant/anti-perspirant is a good idea for your armpits, but it might be best not to use one all the time. The chemicals they contain may be absorbed by your body and some people think these aren't healthy. Try going without a deodorant on days when you're relaxing at home, and don't use one overnight.

# Front to back

Your anus is pretty germy. And if the germs are spread to your vagina and urinary tube, they can cause infections. To avoid this happening, always wipe, wash and dry your genitals from front to back. Use mild soap but no deodorants or perfume here, as they can irritate your skin badly.

Dry here first.

Finish drying here.

# Normal or not?

Remember that the fluid from your vagina is healthy and cleansing. There is more of it at some times than others and its colour can change from clear to milky-white. It's only a problem if it starts to make you itch, burn or smell. This means you may have an infection or an allergic reaction and you need to go to the doctor. The doctor may be able to diagnose the problem from your description, without examining you.

# From the neck up

As if things like breasts and periods weren't enough to worry about, most girls get a bit self-conscious about their faces too. Almost everyone has spots at some time or another, and lots of people get greasy hair.

## Too much grease

Everyone's skin produces a kind of oil called sebum. Without it, your skin and hair would dry out. But the huge changes in your hormone levels, especially in testosterone, can send sebum production out of control. Result: spots and greasy hair. Some people's hair gets so greasy they have to wash it every day.

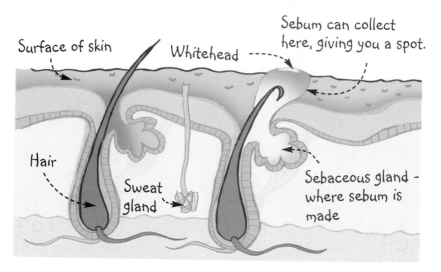

Surface of skin

Whitehead

Sebum can collect here, giving you a spot.

Hair

Sweat gland

Sebaceous gland - where sebum is made

# Dealing with spots

Different people swear by different spot remedies. The best thing is to find out which works best for you.

Wash your face twice a day with mild, unperfumed or antiseptic soap. Use warm water and your bare hands.

Try one of the spot treatments you can buy from the chemist's.

Use as few beauty products as possible if you're in a spotty phase. This includes make-up, although medicated concealer sticks can give good camouflage for just one or two spots.

Keep your hands and nails clean, and don't play with your spots.

Eat a healthy diet. Many people believe that certain foods give them spots, although experts haven't found any evidence for this.

If your spots are really bad, don't put up with them – ask your pharmacist or doctor what to do.

# Squeezing

It probably doesn't do much harm to squeeze the odd spot, but there are a few precautions to take if you do.

* Wash your hands first.
* Use your fingers, not your nails.
* Only squeeze blackheads or whiteheads, nothing red or angry.
* Stop if nothing happens, or if clear fluid or blood comes out.
* Dab on an antiseptic, such as tea tree oil, afterwards.
* Wash your hands again.

# How boys' bodies work

Boys have to go through lots of growing-up changes too. Here you can find out what happens to their bodies so that they can eventually be fathers. Like girls, boys are physically able to produce children much sooner than they are able to look after them.

## Boys' sex organs

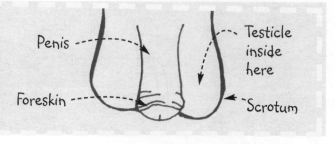

Penis --- Testicle inside here

Foreskin --- Scrotum

Boys' sex organs grow larger at puberty, just like girls' do. And they grow pubic hair too.

The end of the penis is very sensitive and is protected by a fold of skin called the foreskin. In some religions, boys have their foreskin cut away in a surgical operation called circumcision.

At puberty, sperm start being made in a boy's two testicles (his balls). Male sex hormones (androgens) are made here too. Full-grown testicles are about the size of small plums.

A boy's testicles hang outside his body, behind his penis, in a pouch of wrinkled skin called the scrotum. The temperature here is just right for sperm production.

The sperm are stored in a coiled tube called the epididymis. This would be 6m (20ft) long if it was unravelled.

Sperm can get to the penis by travelling along tubes called sperm ducts.

On the way, the sperm are mixed with fluids to make semen. One fluid, which gives the sperm energy, comes from the seminal vesicles. Another fluid, from the prostate gland, helps the sperm to move.

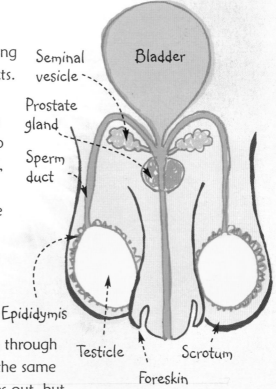

Seminal vesicle

Bladder

Prostate gland

Sperm duct

Epididymis

Testicle

Foreskin

Scrotum

Semen leaves the penis through a hole at the end. It's the same hole where urine comes out, but muscles around the bladder make sure that urine and semen never come out at the same time.

# Hygiene

A white, creamy substance called smegma is made under a boy's foreskin and this helps the skin slide back smoothly. Boys have to wash their penis carefully every day to make sure smegma doesn't build up and get smelly or infected.

# Boys have worries too

Don't think that growing up is a walkover for boys. They can get just as anxious and embarrassed as girls do about the changes they're going through.

## Squeaky voice

As boys grow up, their voice box (larynx) gets bigger and this makes their voice go deeper. While this is happening, a boy's voice can suddenly break into a squeak while he's talking. It's only the muscles of his voice box getting out of control for a moment, but it can be very embarrassing.

la! la!
la!
la!
eek!

## When to shave?

Getting a moustache and beard is one of the last changes to happen to boys. They can feel self-conscious because the hair is quite soft to begin with, and it may not grow evenly, so that they have some hairless patches.

Then, they have to decide when to start shaving and learn how to do it without cutting themselves.

## Size anxieties

Am I tall enough? Are my shoulders broad enough? Am I muscley enough? And (worst of all) is my penis big enough? These are the main anxieties. But there's no "right" size or shape for boys any more than for girls. Everyone is different.

## Breasts?

Some boys worry that they're changing sex because their breasts feel tender and swell up. But this doesn't last long. Once their hormones settle down, the "breasts" disappear.

## Other embarrassments

For a man's penis to fit inside a woman's vagina during sex, it first has to swell, get hard and point upwards. This is called an erection and it happens when extra blood flows into the penis. Boys often have erections at inconvenient moments and it can be especially awkward if the erection won't go down.

While a boy is asleep, he may have what's called a wet dream – an erection and then an orgasm. An orgasm is the moment when semen squirts (ejaculates) out of his penis. This is only his body getting used to its new way of working, but it can be embarrassing to stain the sheets.

# Problems to avoid

As you get older, you could come across some tricky situations. Here are a few of the issues you might have to deal with.

## Drugs

Drugs include alcohol and nicotine (in tobacco) as well as drugs that are illegal (against the law). These include cannabis, ecstasy, crack, cocaine, poppers and magic mushrooms. They are taken in different ways: swallowed, sniffed, smoked or injected, and have different effects. They can all be hugely damaging to a user's health and relationships. And it's easy to become dependent on drugs, physically or mentally, so it becomes very hard to give them up. Some drugs, such as glues, lighter gases and aerosols, which people sniff or spray into their mouths, can even kill the very first time someone uses them.

\* Most heavy smokers die of smoking.

\* Many cannabis-users suffer from depression.

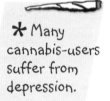

\* Binge drinking can damage your developing brain.

## What is safe sex?

Safe sex doesn't just mean using contraception to avoid pregnancy. If someone has an infection in their sex organs, they can pass it on during sex. Many sexually transmitted infections (STIs) can be cured if treated early, but some can be very serious or even life-threatening – HIV, for example. Using a condom gives some protection against most STIs.

# Body image

It's natural to want to look good, but unrealistic to try to look like a celebrity. Celebrities often look the way they do because they spend vast amounts of time and money on their appearance, and diet and exercise excessively. In any case, people don't necessarily want their girlfriend or boyfriend to look like a star. Different people like different body types and looks.

# Bullying

If you're being bullied, don't suffer alone. Talk about it with an adult you trust. They may be able to help you decide what to do, or even help you find a way to stop the bullying. And remember, it's not your fault – no one deserves to be bullied.

# The right to say no

Sometimes, people try to persuade or even force someone to do things they are too young to do, or that are unhealthy, illegal or just wrong. This could include smoking, drinking, or having sexual contact with them. If anyone puts pressure on you in this way, tell them to stop – they don't have the right to do this, and you have the right to say no. You can also tell an adult you trust what has happened.

# Index

Photographic manipulation: Nick Wakeford.

First published in 2006 by Usborne Publishing Ltd. Usborne House, 83-85 Saffron Hill, London EC1N 8RT, England. www.usborne.com Copyright © 2006 Usborne Publishing Ltd. The name Usborne and the devices ⊕ ♀ are Trade Marks of Usborne Publishing Ltd. All rights reserved. No part of this publication may be reproduced, stored in a retrieval system or transmitted in any form or by any means, electronic, mechanical, photocopying, recording or otherwise, without the prior permission of the publisher. Printed in China.